**For Windows**

---

# super short cuts!

---

*The fastest, easiest way to do it!*

**Expanded edition teaches
essentials *plus* shortcuts!**

# MICROREF®

Educational Systems, Inc.
Northbrook, IL 60062

Product Number S327

99 98 97    4 3 2 1

Printed in the United States of America

# Welcome to Super Shortcuts! . . .

...the speediest guide to computer software. Our goal is to save you time. This guide provides the fastest, easiest ways to run your software program with the fewest number of keystrokes.

This guide contains two parts. The first part is **Outlook 97 Essentials at a Glance** where you can review basic software tasks, necessary concepts, and exciting new features. The second part presents a complete **Shortcut Reference** to the program.

We encourage you to read the first part of this guide page by page. If you are an experienced user, you will gain a fresh perspective on the software with plenty of hidden shortcuts to speed your work. If you are new to this program, the first part of this guide will give you a well-rounded introduction and explain the basic concepts behind the commands.

In addition, glance through the **Shortcut Reference** in the second part of this guide to discover hidden shortcuts not found on menus. You will find time-saving keyboard and mouse tricks that speed you through your work. Also scan the reference section for the most useful icons and learn how they work.

To further speed your work, use the comprehensive **Contents** and **Index** pages to look up quick alternatives to commands you use day in and day out. Finally, to review basic program concepts, study the **It Helps to Know** section at the end of this guide.

## CONTENTS

# Outlook 97 Essentials at a Glance

The **Outlook 97 Essentials at a Glance** section of this guide is a learning tool.

Read through the following procedures for an introduction to basic Outlook tasks. This tour helps you understand the capabilities of Outlook's various components then walks you step-by-step through practical daily procedures.

These procedures provide a broad overview to Outlook that includes specific tasks, necessary concepts, and exciting new features. Whether you're seeking an overall understanding of the program, gaining insights into special aspect of procedures, learning about entirely new additions to the program, or using this guide as a daily reference, this section has something new for you.

## OFFICE FEATURES

## SHORTCUT BAR

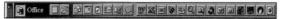

*The Shortcut Bar normally appears at the top of your screen. If you installed Office 97 using the Typical Installation option, this Shortcut Bar will appear only if you installed it in Office 95. If the Shortcut Bar does not appear, rerun Setup from the Office 97 CD to install it.*

*You can view the Shortcut Bar in a window and display different shortcuts at one time.*

**View shortcuts in a window** . . . . . . . . `DRAG` background
*When you move the Shortcut Bar off the top of your screen, it appears in a resizable window. If you display multiple Shortcut Bars (see below), they appear clearly labeled in this window.*

**Resize shortcut window** . . . . . . . . . . . . . . . `DRAG` border
*Drag the window's border to resize and reshape a shortcut window.*

**View different Shortcut Bars**

1. `RCLICK` background

2. `CLICK` toolbar name

*If there is no background space in the Shortcut Bar on which to right-click, then right-click on the vertical pane just before the first button. Shortcut Bars include Office, Desktop, QuickShell, Favorites,*

---

*Programs, and Accessories. If you select multiple*
*Shortcut Bars, a button representing each Shortcut*
*Bar appears on the current Shortcut Bar.*

## Get help

1. in title bar
2. **Contents** and **I**ndex

## Add/remove buttons

1. in title bar
2. **C**ustomize
3. **Buttons** tab

*You can add buttons to open documents that you use*
*frequently. Drag the document icon from the*
*Windows Explorer window to the Buttons tab.*

## Show/hide ToolTips

1. in title bar
2. **C**ustomize
3. **View** tab
4. **S**how ToolTips

## Button size

1. in title bar
2. **C**ustomize
3. **View** tab
4. **L**arge buttons

## Hide Shortcut Bar at Windows startup

1. in title bar

**2. E**x**it**

**3. No** button

*This permanently removes the Shortcut Bar from automatically displaying. To display the Shortcut Bar, open "Program Files\Microsoft Office\Office\Microsoft Office Shortcut Bar."*

### Display Shortcut Bar at Windows
**startup** . . . . . . . . . . . . . . . . . . . . . . . . . . . . . . . `DRAG` icon

*Use this procedure if you have previously followed the preceding procedure to hide the Shortcut Bar. Use Windows Explorer or My Computer to copy the "Program Files\Microsoft Office\Office\Microsoft Office Shortcut Bar" icon to the "\Windows\Start Menu\Programs\StartUp" folder.*

## OFFICE ASSISTANT

*The Office Assistant starts automatically by default in your Office applications.*

**Get rid of the Assistant** . . . . . . . . . . . . . . . . . . . . . . . `✕`

**Get the Assistant back again** . . . . . . . . . . . . . . . . . . . `❓`

### Tell the Assistant when to pop-up
**automatically** . . . . . . . . . . . . . . `RCLICK` title bar, **O**ptions

*To turn off the Office Assistant, clear all options.*

### Open the Assistant or the Index when you press F1

1. `RCLICK` title bar

2. **O**ptions

3. **Respond to F**1 **key**

---

**Use a different Office Assistant character**

1. `RCLICK` title bar
2. Choose Assistant

**Open Help**.................. **Help, Contents and Index**

*You can also set F1 to open Help instead of the Office Assistant as described above.*

## GETTING STARTED

*Outlook is a program that helps you keep track of personal information such as your calendar, contacts, tasks, journal, and notes. You can use Outlook to read and send e-mail as well as manage files and folders on your computer.*

*The information you access in Outlook is your personal information, since you access it through your user profile. If several people use your computer, you can create several user profiles and have Outlook prompt users for which profile to use when they start up Outlook.*

*The Outlook Bar is a vertical pane on the left of the Outlook window. Click on the Outlook button to view and edit personal information. Click on the Mail button to work with e-mail. Click on the Other button to manage files on your computer.*

## START AND EXIT

### Start Outlook from the Windows Start menu

1. Ctrl Esc
2. <u>P</u>rograms
3. 🖀Microsoft Outlook

Start from desktop icon . . . . . . . . . . . . . 2CLICK □  Outlook

**Start from Office Shortcut Bar** . . . . . . . . . . `CLICK` button

*Click a button depending on what you want to do
when you start Outlook. For example, you can display
a new mail message or task. Following are just some
of the buttons on the Office Shortcut Bar that start
Outlook:*

**Create a fax or e-mail message** . . . . . . . . . . . . . . . . . . .

**Create an appointment** . . . . . . . . . . . . . . . . . . . . . . . . . .

**Create a task** . . . . . . . . . . . . . . . . . . . . . . . . . . . . . . . . . .

**Start Outlook when you start Windows**

1. Ctrl Esc
2. **S**ettings, **T**askbar
3. **Start Menu Programs** tab
4. **A**dd button
5. B**r**owse button
6. `2CLICK` Outlook icon

*Programs and documents in the StartUp folder start
automatically. To start Windows without starting these
items, press **Shift** when the Windows logo appears.*

**Create another user profile**

1. Ctrl Esc
2. **S**ettings, **C**ontrol Panel
3. `2CLICK` Mail and Fax icon
4. **S**ervices tab
5. **S**how Profiles button
6. **G**eneral tab

---

7. A**d**d button

8. Follow prompts to configure services

## Have Outlook ask you for the user profile at startup

1. **T**ools, **O**ptions

2. **General** tab

3. **P**rompt for a profile to be used

*If you want Outlook to automatically use a particular
user profile at startup, in step 3 select **"Always use
this profile"** and select a profile.*

Exit Outlook . . . . . . . . . . . . . . . . . . . . . . . . . . . . . . . . . Alt F4

## SWITCH BETWEEN COMPONENTS

*Outlook components include Inbox, Calendar, Contacts, Tasks,
Journal, Notes, Sent Items, Outbox, Deleted Items, and My
Computer.*

Go to component using menu . . . . . . . . . . . . . . . . . . . . . . **Go**

Using shortcut key . . . . . . . . . . . . . . . . . . . . . . . . . . . Ctrl Y

Using Outlook Bar . . . . . . . . . . . . . . . . . . . . . . CLICK icon
*The Outlook Bar is the vertical pane on the left of the
window.*

## Show small icons in Outlook Bar

1. RCLICK bar background

2. S**m**all icons

*The Outlook Bar is the vertical pane on the left of the
window. This procedure fits all component icons in
the Outlook Bar so you can select any icon without
having to scroll the Outlook Bar.*

Widen Outlook Bar . . . . . . . . . . . . . . . . . . . . DRAG border

---

**Hide Outlook Bar**. . . . . . . . . . . . . . . . . . <u>V</u>iew, <u>O</u>utlook Bar
*Make more room on your screen. Repeat to redisplay.*

## CHANGE VIEWS

*Each component in Outlook comes with several useful ways of looking at the information (views). All views are based on one of five basic types: table, timeline, day/week/month, cards, and icons. See the **Shortcut Reference** section at the end of this guide to review how to move around table, day/week/month, and card views.*

**Select a view** . . . . . . . . . . . . . . . . . . . . . <u>V</u>iew, Current <u>V</u>iew
*You may also select a view directly from the drop down list on the toolbar.*

**Customize current view** . . . . . . . . . . . . <u>V</u>iew, Form<u>a</u>t View

**Create a view**. . . . . . . . . . . . . . . . . . . . . <u>V</u>iew, <u>D</u>efine Views
*First, select the Outlook component, such as Tasks or Notes, in which to create the view.*

**Sort table column**. . . . . . . . . . . . . `CLICK` column heading
*This rearranges all items row by row to sort in ascending order by that column. To sort in descending order, click the column heading again.*

**Widen table column**. . . . . . . . . . . . . . . . `DRAG` right edge
of column heading

**Widen table column to fit longest item in a field**. . . . . . . . . `2CLICK` right edge of column heading

**Remove field in table view** . . . . . . . . . . . . . . `DRAG` column heading off screen

---

*You may also right-click the column heading and
select **R**emove This Column.*

**Add field in table view** . . . . . . . . . . . . . . **V**iew, Field **C**hooser
`DRAG ` *the field from the Field Chooser dialog box
to the field column headings in the view.*

## SET UP CATEGORIES

*Categories are an important feature to consider when you set
up and begin organizing your office around Outlook. Use
categories to cross-reference any type of office item.*

*For example, create a category for a particular project, say
Project X. Later, you can view a list of all messages, tasks, and
correspondence related to Project X, and even add up the time
you spent on the project using Outlook's Journal. Also using
Journal, you can quickly retrieve an item (such as a mail
message or a task) related to a category (say Project X)
because Journal keeps a shortcut to the item to which it refers.*

*You can view related items using the **V**iew, **C**urrent **V**iew, By
**C**ategory command within any Outlook component.*

*You can assign more than one category to an Outlook item.
For example, a client can be a Hot Contact as well as a
Supplier.*

*Outlook provides a Master Category List to which you can add
your own categories. The default Master Category List includes
the following:*

Business
Competition
Favorites
Gifts
Goals/Objectives
Holidays

Holiday Cards
Hot Contacts
Ideas
International
Key Customer
Miscellaneous
Personal
Phone Calls
Status
Strategies
Suppliers
Time & Expenses
VIP
Waiting

## Add categories

1. **E**dit, **Categories**
2. **M**aster Category List button
3. Type new category
4. **A**dd button
5. **OK** button

## Assign an item to a category

1. `RCLICK` item
2. **Categories**
3. Check categories
4. **OK** button

*For each **Available category** that you check, the categories for the current item appear at the top of this dialog box.*

**View all items related to a category**

1. Ctrl Shift F
2. At Look for, select **Any type of Outlook item**
3. **More Choices** tab
4. **Categories** button
5. Check categories, **OK** button
6. Find **Now** button

*This searches for items in all Outlook components (messages, tasks, notes, etc.) Found items appear at the bottom of the dialog box.*

## CUSTOMIZE OUTLOOK

**Customize with assistance**

1. **Help, Contents and Index**
2. **Index** tab
3. Type **Getting Results – Customize Office**
4. **Display** button

*Outlook presents a list of customizing options that you should consider as you set up Outlook to work for you. You can customize Office Assistant, Outlook, Mail, Calendar, and Other Item settings.*

## SET APPOINTMENTS IN THE CALENDAR

*Use the Calendar to schedule your appointments, meetings, and events.*

*An appointment is time you block out of your calendar that you reserve for a personal activity such as a phone call, doctor's visit, or vacation. A meeting is an appointment where you invite others. An event is an activity such as a birthday, holiday, or business trip that does not block out time on your calendar. Rather it displays a banner on the day(s) of the event.*

*Outlook reminds you of appointments by displaying a reminder before the appointment. For example, when you create an appointment, you can have Outlook display a reminder 15 minutes before the appointment.*

### WORKING IN DAY/WEEK/MONTH VIEW

*For further shortcuts on viewing and moving between dates, see the **Shortcut Reference** section at the end of this guide.*

Select a view . . . . . . . . . . . . . . . . . . . . . . <u>V</u>iew, Current <u>V</u>iew

*You may also select a view directly from the drop down list on the toolbar.*

View day, week, or month . . . . . . . . . . . . 🔲, 🔲, 🔲

*First, select Day/Week/Month view and maximize window size to see all these options.*

Go to today. . . . . . . . . . . . . . . . . . . . . . . . . . . . . . . . 🔲

Go to any day . . . . . . . . . . . . . . . . . . . . . . . . . . . . . Ctrl G

*You may also click on a date in the Month pane.*

**Go to next/previous appointment** . . . . . . . . . . Tab/Shift Tab

## CREATING AN APPOINTMENT
*When you create an appointment, make sure to specify "Busy,"*
*"Free," "Tentative," or "Out of Office" so that other users*
*on the network can schedule meetings with you. You can also*
*specify that an appointment is "Private."*

**Create an appointment.** . . . . . . . . . . . . . . . . . . . . . **Ctrl Shift K**
*Use this method to create a new appointment from*
*any component.*

**Create an appointment from Calendar** . . . . . . . . . . . **Ctrl N**
*First, you can select time the appointment will start*
*or drag to select block of time the appointment will*
*cover if working in Day view.*

**Create a recurring appointment**
   1. Calendar
   2. New Recurring Appointment
*First, select a date and time. A recurring appointment*
*repeats on a regular basis, such as a meeting that*
*occurs every other Friday at 2 p.m.*

**Finish creating appointment** . . . . . . . . . . . . . . . . . . . . . **Alt S**

**View active appointments**
   1. View, Current View
   2. Active Appointments view
*Appointments have a picture of a calendar. Meetings*
*have a picture of a person's head.*

**View recurring appointments**
   1. View, Current View
   2. Recurring Appointments view

---

**View an appointment** . . . . . . . . . . . `2CLICK` appointment

**Print appointments** . . . . . . . . . . . . . . . . . . . . . . . . . . . . . **Ctrl P**
*Outlook will ask you for a date range and give you a choice of printouts: Daily, Weekly, Monthly, or Tri-fold.*

**Delete an appointment**
 1. `CLICK` appointment
 2. **Ctrl D**

**Undo deletion** . . . . . . . . . . . . . . . . . . . . . . . . . . . . . . . **Ctrl Z**
*You must undo before moving to another Outlook component.*

### CREATING A MEETING
*You can invite attendees to your meeting and request resources (conference rooms). Attendee names appear in the "To" box and resources appear in the "Location" box. Outlook passes out invitations and resource requests by e-mail. When an attendee responds, Outlook keeps track of the responses for you.*

**Schedule meeting from Calendar**
 1. **Ctrl Shift Q**
 2. **To:** . . . button
 3. Select from **Show Names**
 4. Select name(s)
 5. **Required, Optional,** or **Resources** button
 6. **OK** button
 7. Type **Subject** and **Location**
 8. **Meeting Planner** tab
 9. **AutoPick** button

---

**10.** `☐ Send`

*First, select time the meeting will start or drag to select block of time the meeting will cover.*

**Schedule meeting from Contacts list . . . . . . . . . . Ctrl Shift G**
*First, select name of person from Contacts list. See steps in procedure above to complete the meeting.*

**Schedule a recurring meeting**
1. <u>C</u>alendar
2. New Re<u>c</u>urring Meeting

**Keep journal of meetings**
1. <u>T</u>ools, <u>O</u>ptions
2. Journal tab
3. Select **Meeting cancellation, Meeting request** and/or **Meeting response**

*Outlook will automatically record a journal entry each time you cancel, request, or respond to a meeting request.*

**View active meetings**
1. <u>V</u>iew, Current <u>V</u>iew
2. **Active Appointments** view

*Appointments have a picture of a calendar. Meetings have a picture of a person's head.*

**View recurring meetings**
1. <u>V</u>iew, Current <u>V</u>iew
2. **Recurring Appointments** view

**View a meeting** . . . . . . . . . . . . . . . . . . . . `2CLICK` meeting
*Double-click on the meeting entry. When you view*
*(open) a meeting, you can make changes and Outlook*
*will notify all attendees.*

### Check conference room

1. `RCLICK` resource

2. Select **Properties**
*This shows you information about the resource.*

### Check responses

1. `2CLICK` meeting

2. **Meeting Planner** tab

3. Check **Show attendee status**

**Reschedule a meeting** . . . . . . . . . . . . `DRAG` appointment
*You can drag the appointment to a new time or date*
*in the Date Navigator. In Day view, drag the left move*
*handle; otherwise drag the entire appointment.*
*Outlook asks you if you would like to automatically*
*notify attendees of the change.*

### Invite more people

1. `2CLICK` meeting

2. **Meeting Planner** tab

3. **Invite Others.** . . . button

4. Select from **Show Names**

5. Select name(s)

6. **Required, Optional,** or **Resources** button

7. **OK** button

8. `Send`

**Make a meeting recur** . . . . . . . . . . . . . . . . . . . . . . . . . . **Ctrl G**

---

*First, view (open) the meeting. Outlook will ask if you wish to notify attendees that the meeting will recur on a regular basis.*

## Cancel a meeting
1. `CLICK` meeting
2. Ctrl D

*If the meeting is a recurring meeting, Outlook asks if you want to cancel the selected occurrence or the entire series. Outlook will ask if you wish to notify attendees that you have canceled the meeting.*

## CREATING AN EVENT
*Events do not block out time on your calendar. Rather, they display a banner for the day or period of days. Sample events are birthdays, anniversaries, holidays, trade shows.*

*Events appear as available days to others who wish to schedule meetings with you (the time is not reserved).*

**Create an event** . . . . . . . . . . . . . . . . . . **Calendar, New Event**
*If desired, first select the day to include in the event.*

## Repeat event on several days
1. `RDRAG` event
2. Copy

*First, set display to View, Week or View, Month. If the event spans several days, this procedure copies it to another day.*

## Create an annual or recurring event
1. Calendar
2. New Recurring Event

---

*After selecting **D**aily, **W**eekly, **M**onthly, or **Y**early and
filling in the dates, select OK. Then type a name for
the event at "Subject."*

## Add holidays automatically

1. **T**ools, **O**ptions
2. **Calendar** tab
3. **Add H**olidays button

*Outlook asks you for a country, then automatically
adds holidays for the country you specify.*

## Delete an event

1. `CLICK` event
2. **Ctrl D**

*If the event is a recurring event, Outlook asks if you
want to delete the selected event or all occurrences.*

## View all events

1. **V**iew, Current **V**iew
2. **Events** view

## View all annual events

1. **V**iew, Current **V**iew
2. **Annual Events** view

## CUSTOMIZING THE CALENDAR WINDOW

## Show a second time zone

1. **T**ools, **O**ptions
2. **Calendar** tab
3. **Time Z**one button
4. Check **S**how additional time zone

---

*The second time zone is visible when you display days in Day/Week/Month view. Use it when you often communicate with colleagues in a different time zone.*

**Show week numbers**

1. **T̲ools, O̲ptions**
2. **Calendar** tab
3. Check **Show wee̲k numbers**

*Outlook adds week numbers to Date Navigator calendars. For example, Day view shows Date Navigator months in the upper-right corner of the screen.*

**Specify tasks to display in TaskPad. . . . . . . . . . . . . . . . . . . . . . . . V̲iew, Tas̲kPad View**
*You must be in Day/Week/Month view. The TaskPad is in the lower-right corner in Day view and Week view. Use this procedure to specify the type of tasks to include in the TaskPad such as All Tasks, Today's Tasks, etc.*

## STORE YOUR CONTACTS

*Use Contacts to store information about people and businesses. You can store general information such as name, address, phone number, fax number, and e-mail address as well as more detailed information such as profession, birthday, and nickname.*

*Outlook helps you dial, e-mail, schedule meetings with, visit the Web site of, and write letters to contacts. Outlook can keep a journal entry of all phone conversations with contacts, so you can review previous calls to specific contacts before contacting them again.*

*Use Word 97 in conjunction with Outlook to print mailing labels or envelopes to all or selected Contacts.*

## CREATING A CONTACT

**Create a contact**........................... Ctrl Shift C
*Use this method to create a new contact from any
component. Outlook automatically adds all contacts
that include an e-mail address to the Outlook
Address Book.*

**Create a contact from Contacts** ................. Ctrl N

**Finish creating contact**........................... Alt S

**Import Personal Address Book**
1. **File, Import** and **Export**
2. Select **Import from Schedule+** or another program or file, **Next**
3. Select **Personal Address Book, Next**
4. Select **Contacts** folder, **Next**
5. **Finish** button

## VIEWING CONTACTS

**Sort contacts** ...... **View, Sort** *or* CLICK column header
*For example, organize contacts by first name, last
name, zip code, or another field. If you click the
column header once, Outlook sorts (alphabetizes)
contacts by that column. If you click the header again,
Outlook sorts contacts in reverse order.*

**Filter contacts**........................... **View, Filter**
*To remove a filter, repeat above procedure and
select* **Clear All** *button.*

---

**Find a contact** .......................... Ctrl Shift F
*Make sure you set **Look for** to Contacts. Contact rows will appear at the bottom of the dialog box. To open the contact, double-click on the desired row.*

**Select a view** ..................... View, Current View
*You may also select a view directly from the drop down list on the toolbar. Choose to view address cards, phone list, by location, etc.*

### CALLING A CONTACT

**Call a contact** ..................................
*First, select name of person from Contacts list. Your computer must have a modem and you must have the capability to switch to voice mode so that you can pick up the phone after Outlook dials.*

*If you select to **Create new Journal Entry when starting new call,** Outlook will create a journal entry that includes the contact information and length of the call. You can add notes about the conversation to the journal entry.*

**Keep journal of calls**

1. Tools, Options

2. Journal tab

3. Select names under **For these contacts**

*Use this procedure to select the names of contacts for which Outlook will automatically record a journal entry each time you AutoDial.*

---

### Show journal for contact

1. `2CLICK` contact

2. **Journal** tab

*This is available if you create journal entries for contacts.*

**Redial** . . . . . . . . . . . . . . . . . . . . . . . . . . . . **Tools, Dial, Redial**
*Outlook keeps a list of the last contacts that you dialed.*

**Call a non-contact** . . . . . . . . . . . . . . . . . . . . . . . **Ctrl Shift D**
*At the dialog box, type the name and number of the person or business and select whether you want to record the call in your journal. At **Contact,** select the down arrow to choose from a list of people you have already called. If you type the name of a contact, Outlook will find that contact's phone number for you.*

### OTHER MEANS OF CONTACT

**Schedule meeting** . . . . . . . . . . . . . . . . . . . . . . . . **Ctrl Shift G**
*First, select name of person from Contacts list.*

**Go to contact's Web page**. . . . . . . . . . . . . . . . . . **Ctrl Shift X**
*You must have the address of the Web Page stored in the information for the contact and you must have Internet access.*

**Create letter**. . . . . . . . . . . **Contacts, New Letter to Contact**
*First, select name of person from Contacts list. Opens Microsoft Word and starts the Letter Wizard. Word fills in the contact name and address information for you.*

---

**Send message** . . . . . . . . Co̱ntacts, New M̱essage to Contact
*First, select name of person from Contacts list.*

**Print contacts.** . . . . . . . . . . . . . . . . . . . . . . . . . . . . . . . . . . Ctrl P
*If desired, first select contacts to print from Contacts
list. Available layouts depend on the current view.*

### Print one label or envelope

1. Start Word 97
2. Ṯools, E̱nvelopes and Labels
3. **Envelopes** tab or **Labels** tab
4. Click Address Book icon
5. Select from S̱how Names
6. Select Contacts
7. **OK** button
8. **P̱rint** button

*Use this procedure to print a label or envelope for
only one contact.*

### Print multiple labels or envelopes

1. Start Word 97
2. Ṯools, Mail M̱erge
3. C̱reate button
4. Select M̱ailing labels or E̱nvelopes
5. G̱et data button
6. Select Use A̱ddress Book
7. Select **Outlook Address Book**
8. **OK** button
9. Follow prompts to set up document

---

*Use this procedure to print form letters or mass
mailing labels or envelopes. To send to a subset of all
the contacts, either use Word 97's Query Options
button during mail merging, or create a separate
Contacts folder before beginning this procedure. To
create a separate folder press **Ctrl Shift E,** type a
name for the new folder, select "Contact Items" after
**Folder Contains,** and OK, then click Contacts from
the Outlook Bar (left side of window), and **Ctrl** drag
selected contacts to the new folder.*

## KEEP A TASK LIST

*Keep a Task List to organize projects into discrete tasks. You
can keep track of any activity you need to perform.*

### CREATING A TASK

**Create task** . . . . . . . . . . . . . . . . . . . . . . . . . . . . . Ctrl Shift K
*Use this method to create a task from any
component.*

**Create task from Tasks** . . . . . . . . . . . . . . . . . . . . . . . Ctrl N

**Create a recurring task** . . . . . . . . . . . . . . . . . . . . . .
*First, create or open a task to set as recurring. Set up
two kinds of recurring tasks: 1) Have Outlook
schedule the next recurring task in the series only
when you mark the current recurring task as
complete, 2) Have a task occur regularly, such as
every second Friday.*

**Finish creating task** . . . . . . . . . . . . . . . . . . . . . . . . . . . Alt S

**Keep journal of tasks**

   1. <u>T</u>ools, <u>O</u>ptions

   2. Journal tab

**3.** Select **Task request** and/or **Task response**
*Outlook will automatically record a journal entry for each request or response.*

**Schedule a task** . . . . . . . `DRAG` task icon to Calendar icon
*Drag the task icon from the Tasks list over to the Calendar icon in the Outlook Bar (left side of screen). Use this procedure to schedule time for working on the task. Outlook creates a new appointment with information about the task filled in for you.*

## VIEWING TASKS

### View active tasks

1. <u>V</u>iew, Current <u>V</u>iew

2. Select **Active Tasks**
*You may also select this view directly from the toolbar.*

### View overdue tasks

1. <u>V</u>iew, Current <u>V</u>iew

2. Select **Overdue Tasks**
*You may also select this view directly from the toolbar.*

### View upcoming tasks

1. <u>V</u>iew, Current <u>V</u>iew

2. Select **Next Seven Days**
*You may also select this view directly from the toolbar.*

## EDITING TASKS

**Edit task** . . . . . . . . . . . . . . . . . . . . . . . . . . . `2CLICK` task icon

**Update hours, billing, contacts, etc.** . . . . . . . . . . . . **Status** tab
*First, create or open a task. Use this procedure to
see if task is completed, to enter the estimated time
to complete (**Total work**), to enter the number of
hours you spent on the task (**Actual work**), to enter
expenses information such as total mileage, billing
information, contacts, and companies involved, and to
view a list of people who requested and received the
task and those with updated copies of assigned tasks
(**Update list**). Outlook converts hours of work to
days based on your **Tools, Options, Tasks/Notes** tab,
**Hours per day** and **Hours per week** settings.*

**Mark task as complete** . . . . . . . . . . . . . . . . . . . . . . . .
*First, create or open a task. Tasks marked as
completed are not deleted since you might wish to
archive them. They appear dimmed and crossed out
in the task list.*

**Delete selected task** . . . . . . . . . . . . . . . . . . . . . . . . . . **Ctrl D**

### ASSIGNING TASKS

**Create task to assign** . . . . . . . . . . . . . . . . . . . . . . . **Ctrl Shift U**
*The person who receives the task request can accept
it, decline it, or assign it to someone else. You can
specify to retain an updated copy of the assigned task,
but you can no longer modify the task.*

**Assign a task** . . . . . . . . . . . . . . . . . . . . . . . . **Task, Assign Task**
*First, create a normal task or open an existing task.*

---

### View tasks you've assigned

1. **View, Current View**
2. Select **Assignment**

*You may also select this view directly from the toolbar.*

### View status of an assigned task . . . . . . . . . . . . . . . **Status** tab

*First, create or open a task. Use this procedure to view a list of people who requested and received the task and those with updated copies of assigned tasks (**Update list**).*

### Reassign task request

1. Open message with task
2. **Task, Assign Task**
3. Type name at **To**
4. **Send** button

*Use this procedure when you receive a task request and you wish to assign the task to someone else or when the recipient has declined the task request. You must open the mail message from your Inbox.*

### Reclaim ownership of declined task

1. Open message with task
2. **Task, Return to Task List**

*Use this procedure when someone has declined a task request and you wish to reclaim ownership of the task. You must open the mail message from your Inbox.*

# RECORD ACTIVITIES IN A JOURNAL

*Use Journal to keep track of your activities over time. With a flexible cross-indexing approach, Journal lets you view activities by type of activity, by contact, by category, or by time. Before Journal logs an activity, however, you must create a journal entry for that activity, often automatically. For example, you can automatically record the time that you spend working in documents (for billing purposes), or automatically track phone conversations and meetings with specific contacts. There is not much that your journal cannot track automatically.*

*Activities that Outlook can record automatically include e-mail messages, meeting cancellations, requests, and responses, and task requests and responses. Outlook only automatically records the activities related to contacts you specify. And Outlook automatically records your time spent on the Office 97 programs Access, Excel, Binder, PowerPoint, and Word.*

*Activities that you must record manually include contacts not initiated by you through your computer (calls you receive), and time you spend on tasks not recorded in the computer. For example, you might manually record a paper letter or magazine that you read.*

*Why use Journal? The real power of Journal is in reviewing previous activities to prepare billing, before calling a contact, or in finding a document or message. For example, you can view all previous activities with a contact before picking up the phone and calling him or her. When you review activities, Outlook gives you a shortcut to the original message, phone call, or document used in the activity. Using the shortcut, you can review and even edit items and documents you worked on without needing to remember where you stored the documents.*

**Set up automatic recording**

 1. **Tools**, **Options**
 2. **Journal** tab

*Journal will only automatically record e-mail, meetings, and assigned tasks for the contacts you specify. Outlook can record certain activities automatically such as sending e-mail, creating or changing a meeting, requesting or responding to a task, calling a contact, or working on an Office 97 document.*

*For example, you can have Outlook track the time that you spend working in Office documents. The journal entry for this activity includes a shortcut that you can click to open the document and a record of the amount of time you spent in the document.*

*In order for automatic journal entries to be useful, you must maintain them. For example, if you are billing for time spent working on a document, open the journal entry and assign a category for that project.*

**Record an activity** . . . . . . . . . . . . . . . . . . . . . . . . . **Ctrl Shift J**

*Use this method to manually create a journal entry no matter what Outlook component is open. For example, you can record a letter you receive in the mail. You must specify the type of activity. The list of activity types includes the following:*

Conversation

Document

E-mail message

Fax

Letter

Meeting

Meeting cancellation

Meeting request

Meeting response

Microsoft Access

Microsoft Excel

Microsoft Office Binder

Microsoft PowerPoint

Microsoft Word

Note

Phone call

Remote session

Task

Task request

Task response

**Record an activity from Journal** . . . . . . . . . . . . . . . . . **Ctrl N**

*Use this method to manually create a journal entry while the Journal component is open.*

**Record current activity** . . . . . . . . . . . . . . . . . . . . . . . **Ctrl J**

*First, open an Outlook item. In many dialog boxes, such as an open mail message or contact, press **Ctrl J** to create a journal entry with information about the open item filled in for you. Journal stores a shortcut to the open item.*

**Time an activity** . . . . . . . . . . . . . . . . . . . . **Start Timer button**

*First, create a journal entry and fill in information about the activity. When you are ready to start the activity, start the timer. Keep the journal entry open in the background so that you can pause, resume, and stop the timer as needed.*

---

**View all activities for a contact** . . . . . . . . . . . . . . **Journal** tab
*First, open the contact's name in the Contact list.*

**Show entries in a timeline**
1. **V**iew
2. **D**ay, *or* **W**eek

*A timeline view requires space on the screen. For
more space, hide the Outlook Bar (* `▓ RCLICK` *
background).*

## JOT DOWN NOTES

*Create Notes to jot down quick reminders and place them on
your screen. Notes do not stick to pages of documents, rather
they stay on the screen where you place them.*

*Use Notes to replace the scraps of notes you normally keep on
your desk, for example: directions, instructions, questions,
ideas, reminders, facts, text to reuse in other documents.*

### CREATING NOTES

**Create a note** . . . . . . . . . . . . . . . . . . . . . . . . . . . . . . **Ctrl Shift N**
*Use this method to create a note from any
component. No matter where you create the note,
Outlook stores it in the Notes folder until you delete
it.*

**Create note from Notes** . . . . . . . . . . . . . . . . . . . . . . . . **Ctrl N**

**Open a note** . . . . . . . . . . . . . . . . . . . . . `2CLICK ▓` note icon
*You can edit the note once you open it. If you have
the Outlook window maximized, previously opened
notes will disappear behind the window. To view all
open notes, minimize or resize the Outlook window.*

**Open several notes**

1. Ctrl `CLICK` each note
2. Ctrl O

Move a note. . . . . . . . . . . . . . . . . . . . . . . . . . `DRAG` title bar

*Outlook remembers this position the next time you open the note.*

Close a note. . . . . . . . . . . . . . . . . . . . . . . . . . . `CLICK` ☒

## MANAGING NOTES

Select a view . . . . . . . . . . . . . . . . . . . . . . . **View, Current View**

*You can view notes as icons or in lists. You may also select a view directly from the drop down list on the toolbar.*

Assign a category . . . . . . . . `RCLICK` note icon, **Categories**

*You can view all component items related to a category by pressing **Ctrl Shift F** and selecting **Any type of Outlook item** from the **Look for** box.*

E-mail a note . . . . . . . . . . . . . . . . . . . . . . . . . . . . . . **Ctrl F**

*First, select note to send. Creates a mail message with an icon that the recipient can double-click to read the note.*

**Copy note text to document** . . . . . . . . . . . . . . . . . `DRAG ▮`

*For example, copy note text into a Word document.*
*First, display the document on the screen and drag*
*the icon for the closed note over to the document.*
*(Make sure the note is closed. If open, it simply*
*remains on the screen.)*

**Change color of a note** . . . . . . . `▮ RCLICK` note icon, **Color**

*This changes the color of both the note when it is*
*open and the closed note icon. Use different*
*colors to organize your notes. If note is*
*already open, to set the color,* `CLICK ▮` *on the* 🗐 *in*
*the upper-left corner of the note.*

**Set note defaults**

  1. **T**ools, **O**ptions
  2. **Tasks/Notes** tab

*Specify the default color, font, show/hide the*
*date/time stamp, and other settings. If you do not*
*display the date/time stamp, Outlook still retains the*
*information. You can redisplay it at any time.*

**Delete a note**. . . . . . . . . . . . . . . . . . . . . . . . . . . . . . . **Del**

*To undelete a note immediately, press **Ctrl Z**.*

## SEND AND RECEIVE MESSAGES

*Use Mail to send and receive faxes and electronic mail.*
*Electronic mail can be network mail and Internet mail.*

### USING MESSAGE FOLDERS

**Show Mail Bar**. . . . . . . . . . . . . . . . . . . . . . . . ▮  Mail  ▮

*This button appears on the Outlook Bar on the left of*
*the Outlook window. Use the Mail Bar to move*
*between component folders in Mail.*

**Go to Inbox** . . . . . . . . . . . . . . . . . . . . . . . . . . . . . **Ctrl Shift I**
*Use this method to go to the Inbox from any
component.*

**Go to Outbox** . . . . . . . . . . . . . . . . . . . . . . . . . . . **Ctrl Shift O**
*Use this method to go to the Outbox from any
component.*

**Go to Sent Items**. . . . . . . . . . . . . . . . . . . . . . . **Go, Sent Items**

**Go to Deleted Items**. . . . . . . . . . . . . . . . **Go, Deleted Items**

**Create journal entry for a message** . . . . . . . . . . . . . . . **Ctrl J**
*First, select or open the message. The journal entry
includes information about the message and a
shortcut to the message.*

**Keep journal of all messages**
1. **Tools, Options**
2. **Journal** tab
3. Check **E-mail message**

**SENDING A MESSAGE**

**Create fax or e-mail** . . . . . . . . . . . . . . . . . . . . . . **Ctrl Shift M**
*Use this method to create a message from any
component.*

**Create fax or e-mail from Mail** . . . . . . . . . . . . . . . . . **Ctrl N**
*Use this method to create a message while in Inbox,
Outbox, Sent Items, or Deleted Items.*

**Create fax** . . . . . . . . . . . . . . . . . . . . . . . . . . . . . **Compose, Fax**
*You must be in Inbox, Outbox, Sent Items, or
Deleted Items and you must have fax software
installed. Not all procedures listed below are available
if you use this method of creating a fax.*

---

**Create using template** . . . . . . . **Compose, Choose Template**
*You must be in Inbox, Outbox, Sent Items, or
Deleted Items. Use this procedure to create a new e-
mail message with a graphic format. This uses
Microsoft Word to add an e-mail message template
such as Flame, High Tech, Ocean, and Urgent.*

**Create using Address Book**
1. **Ctrl Shift B**
2. **Ctrl** `CLICK` to select recipients
3. **Ctrl N**

**Create and send a document**
1. **Ctrl Shift H**
2. Select template, **OK**
3. Select **Send the document to someone**
4. Fill in address
5. **Document** tab, type document
6. **Options** tab, set options
7. **Send** button
*You can create a Word, Excel, Excel chart, or
PowerPoint document.*

**Mail existing file**
1. `RCLICK` file
2. Se**nd** To
3. **Mail Recipient**
*First **Go, My Computer** to select the file. This sends a
copy of the file embedded as an icon. The file is not
linked to the original. The file can be any type of
document (such as a workbook or picture) or a
program.*

**Fax existing document**

   1. `RCLICK` document

   2. Se_n_d To

   3. Fax Recipient

*First __Go__, __My Computer__ to select the file.*

**Mail document from within Word**

   1. _F_ile, Sen_d_ To

   2. _M_ail Recipient

**Fax document from within Word**

   1. _F_ile, Sen_d_ To

   2. _F_ax Recipient

**Address fax or e-mail**

   1. To_:_ . . . button

   2. Select from **Show Names**

   3. `2CLICK` each name, **OK**

*First, display message on your screen. You can select one or more recipients. Separate names with a semicolon (;). The recipients can be on other e-mail systems.*

*The **To** box requires a recipient's name or e-mail address. If you type a name, Outlook will match it with the closest entry in your Personal Address Book. For example, type Edit;Jeffrey;Melinda and press **Tab**, and Outlook will replace it with Edit Corporation;Jeffrey Kimball;Melinda Yu. To mail to a personal distribution list, select **Personal Address Book** from **Show Names**, then select a boldfaced group name. To create a personal distribution list, see **Address Books** section below.*

*The **From, Cc, Bcc,** and **Subject** boxes are optional.
"From" allows you to send a message on someone else's
behalf (you need appropriate permissions to do so). To
view the From field, select **View, From Field.** "Cc" stands
for Carbon Copy and "Bcc" stands for Blind Carbon
Copy. Names in the Cc box are visible to other
recipients, whereas names in the Bcc field are not visible
to other recipients. To view the Bcc field, select **View,
Bcc Field.***

**Insert a file.** . . . . . . . . . . . . . . . . . . . . . . . . . . . . . . . . . . . .
*First, display message on your screen. In addition to the
attached file, you can type text or attach other files. The
attached file is a copy of the original and is not linked to
the original. The file can be any type of document (such
as a workbook or a picture) or a program.*

### Insert and link a document

1. **Ctrl Shift M** to create message
2. Place cursor in text box
3. **Insert, Object**
4. Create from **File**
5. Select **File**
6. Check **Link**
7. If desired, check **Display As Icon**

*Recipients can double-click a linked document to modify
the original. For recipients to share a linked document,
they must be able to access your network and your
network must support UNC addresses (e.g.,
\\Data\Documents\ Review.doc). To edit a link, select
object and use **Edit, Links.***

---

## Insert your signature

1. Position cursor at end

2. Insert, AutoSignature

*Outlook inserts the AutoSignature you created in the* **Setting Up Mail** *section below. In that section, you can select to have Outlook automatically add your signature to messages. You can be in any item other than a Note to insert your signature.*

## Set fax send options

1. Tools, Microsoft Fax Tools

2. Options

3. Message tab

*Use this procedure to set when faxes should be sent and to select, create, or modify a fax cover page. You must have Microsoft Fax installed.*

**Send message** ....................  *or* **Ctrl Enter**

*First, make sure e-mail or fax message is open on your screen. By default, Outlook will store e-mail in the Outbox until you connect to your mail delivery service. By default, Outlook tries to send faxes right away. If the fax message does not connect and send correctly, you will receive an "Undeliverable" message in your Inbox, which you can open and resend using the* **Send Again** *button.*

---

## VOTING BY E-MAIL

### Add voting buttons to e-mail

1. Create message
2. **Options** tab
3. Check **Use voting buttons**
4. Select ▼ or type button text
5. Check **Save sent messages to**

*Select from: Approve;Reject, Yes;No, and Yes;No;Maybe.*
*To add your own button text, type in text box. Example:*
*Pizza;Lasagna;Sandwiches. Buttons do not appear in the*
*message text while you are creating the message.*

**Vote by e-mail** . . . . . . . . . . . . . . . . . . CLICK voting button
*All the recipient has to do is to click a button and*
*return the message. Outlook tracks voting responses*
*for you.*

### Collect voting responses

1. 2CLICK your message
2. **Tracking** tab

*First, look in Sent Items or wherever you designated*
*Outlook to store the original message.*

### Automatically delete responses

1. **Tools, Options**
2. **E-mail** tab
3. Check **Delete receipts and blank responses after processing**

*This will automatically delete any voting response*
*where the person answered your question, but did*
*not type additional comments. Outlook will first*
*record the response on the original message tally.*

## RECEIVING FAXES

You must have Microsoft Fax installed.

### Receive faxes automatically

1. **T**ools, Microsoft Fa**x** Tools
2. **O**ptions
3. **Modem** tab
4. Select modem, **Properties** button
5. Select **A**nswer after
6. Set number of **rings, OK**

*The fax sets itself to answer all incoming calls right away and whenever you start up Outlook. To turn off automatic answering, repeat this procedure and select* **Don't answer** *in Step 5.*

### Set up phone line primarily to receive voice calls

1. **T**ools, Microsoft Fa**x** Tools
2. **O**ptions
3. **Modem** tab
4. Select modem, **Properties** button
5. Select **M**anual, OK

*Microsoft Fax will display a message on the screen whenever the phone rings and asks if you want to receive a fax at that time.*

### Request fax from fax server

1. **T**ools, Microsoft Fa**x** Tools
2. **R**equest a Fax

*Follow instructions in Request a Fax wizard.*

**View outgoing faxes**

1. Tools, Microsoft Fax Tools

2. Show Outgoing Faxes

## RECEIVING E-MAIL (ONE USER)

*Use the following procedures if you are the only person accessing the mailbox. If two or more people (or computers) access the same mailbox, see the next section.*

**Check for new mail** . . . . . . . . . . . . . . . . . . . . . . . . . . . . . **F5**

*This procedure downloads new mail from the current mail delivery service and deletes the original copies on the mail delivery service. To select and connect to a mail delivery service, use the next procedure. If you are connected to a Microsoft Exchange server, the server automatically delivers mail to your Microsoft Exchange Server mailbox. If you dial in to a Microsoft Exchange network, you should send and receive messages to an offline folder (use Tools, Synchronize when not connected directly to the network).*

**Check for new mail on a specific service**

1. Tools

2. Check for New Mail On

**Check remote mail**

1. Tools, Remote Mail, Connect

2. Check service you want, Next

3. Select what to send and receive, Finish

*Use this procedure to have your modem call up your Internet Service Provider to send and download Internet mail. You must previously configure dial-up networking on your computer using Windows. New*

messages will appear in your Inbox, and Outlook will
disconnect automatically for you.

## RECEIVING E-MAIL (MORE THAN ONE USER)
If two or more people and/or computers use the same mailbox,
use the following four procedures to check your mail. These
special procedures are necessary because Outlook deletes the
original messages from the mail delivery service once you have
downloaded them, thus making them unavailable for another
user of the mailbox or from another remote computer.

### Check headers only
1. Tools, Remote Mail, Connect
2. Check service you want, Next
3. Select Do only the following
4. Check Retrieve new message headers
5. Finish button

Once you download the headers, use the following
procedures to mark the actual messages to download.
This is useful if two or more people and/or
computers use the same mail box.

**View mail tools. . . . . . . . Tools, Remote Mail, Remote Tools**
Use the Remote Tools to mark message headers that
you downloaded during the above procedure. Marked
message headers tell Outlook which messages to
download.

**Mark mail to retrieve, copy, or delete. . . .** 2CLICK header
or **Mark to Retrieve** button
or **Mark to Retrieve a Copy** button
or **Delete** button

First, select message(s) to mark. Use buttons on the
Remote Toolbar to mark, unmark, and delete. Select

---

the **Mark to Retrieve** button to retrieve the original message and delete it from the mail delivery service. Select the **Mark to Retrieve a Copy** button if you want to leave the original message on the mail delivery service after you download it. Select the **Delete** button to delete the message on the mail delivery service without downloading it.

## Download marked mail only

1. **Connect** button
2. Check service you want, **Next**
3. Select **Do only the following**
4. Check each header name you marked, **Finish**

First, use the preceding three procedures to mark messages to retrieve, retrieve a copy, and delete. Use the button on the Remote Toolbar to connect.

## RESPONDING TO E-MAIL

**Reply to sender** ............................... Ctrl R

*Selected or open message. Replies to the sender of the mail message currently open on your screen. This does not send your reply to other recipients of the original message.*

**Reply to sender and all recipients** ............ Ctrl Shift R

*Selected or open message.*

**Forward a message** ........................... Ctrl F

*Selected or open message.*

**Forward your messages automatically**

1. **T**ools

2. O**u**t of Office Assistant

*Use this procedure if you will be on vacation and you want someone else to handle your e-mail or if you are temporarily at another location and want to access your e-mail through another account. You must use Microsoft Exchange Server, be connected, and have the Emsuix.ecf add-in that contains the Out of Office Assistant installed and loaded (checked). To install and load an add-in, use **Tools, Options, General** tab, **A**dd-**In Manager** button, and **I**nstall button.*

**Automatically reply to messages**

1. **T**ools

2. O**u**t of Office Assistant

3. I am currently out of the Office

*This procedure is useful if you would like to reply to all messages that you have changed mailboxes or will be gone for a period of time and suggest that senders write to a different address. Check **AutoReply only once to each sender with the following text** and type text. See above note to install this add-in.*

## FLAGGING MESSAGES

*Flag messages that you send or receive to indicate what to do with the message.*

*For example, specific flags require a phone call, follow up, forwarding, reading, replying, or reviewing. Some flags indicate not to forward or respond.*

**Flag open message** . . . . . . . . . . . . . . . . . . ▼ or **Ctrl Shift G**
*First, make sure message is open on your screen
while you are reading it or before sending it. Select
the type of flag and, optionally, add a due date from
the pop-up calendar. This procedure adds a red
message flag to the message that appears in the Inbox
or Outbox.*

**Change flag in open message** . . . . . . . . . ▼ or **Ctrl Shift G**
*Mail message must be open on the screen. To delete
the message flag, click on the **Clear Flag** button. To
turn the flag white rather than red, select **Completed**.*

### Flag selected message

1. **RCLICK** message
2. **Flag Message**

*First, open the Inbox or Sent Mail window and
highlight the message that you wish to flag. This
procedure automatically marks the message with a
red "Followup" flag.*

### Mark flagged message as complete

1. **RCLICK** message
2. **Flag Complete**

*First, open the Inbox or Sent Mail window and
highlight the message that you have already acted
upon. This turns the flag white, rather than red.*

### Delete message flag

1. **RCLICK** message
2. **Clear Message Flag**

*First, open the Inbox or Sent Mail window and
highlight the message whose flag you want to remove.*

---

### Boldface message as unread

1. `RCLICK` message

### 2. Mark as Unread

*First, open the Inbox window and highlight the message that you have already read, but want to remain bold (unread).*

## SETTING UP MAIL

### Enable or disable Word as your e-mail editor

1. Tools, Options

### 2. E-mail tab

*By default, Word is your e-mail editor. If you do not need the added features of using Word and it takes a long time to load, you can disable it.*

### Set up an AutoSignature

1. Tools, AutoSignature

*First, go to the Inbox. An AutoSignature is your personalized signature. You might want to use this signature to show your name, position, organization, phone number, fax number, e-mail address, mailing address, and other information.*

*You can select to have Outlook add this signature automatically to the end of every new message. To format text, select text and then a Font and/or Paragraph format.*

*This procedure varies depending whether you use Word as your e-mail editor. If you use Word, first create the AutoSignature (it can be a graphic such as an AutoShape) in a mail message. Select your AutoSignature and then select Tools, AutoSignature.*

*If you do not use Word as your e-mail editor, create or copy and paste the AutoSignature in the dialog box.*

## Set up automatic formatting for your replies
1. **Tools, Options**
2. **Reading** tab

*Formats your text in messages when you reply to a message. You usually set up automatic formatting for replies in order to distinguish your comments from those of others. That way, it is easier to keep track of the responses of different people in long mail threads.*

## ADDRESS BOOKS
*Use the Address Book window to add or delete names or to create a message.*

## Create message from address book
1. **Ctrl Shift B**
2. **Ctrl** **CLICK** to select message recipients
3. **Ctrl N**

*Use this method to open the address book from any component. This displays the names in the default address book. The default address book when you install Outlook is the Outlook Address Book, created from your contact list. To show names in a different address book, select a different address book at **Show Names.***

---

### Address a new message

1. Create message
2. To, . . . button
3. Select from **Show Names**
4. `2CLICK` each name
5. **OK** button

*This opens a variation of the address book. You can create new entries from this screen and view other address books such as personal distribution lists (see procedure below to create).*

### Modify address book. . . . . . . . . . . . . . . . . . . . . . . Ctrl Shift B

*Use this method to open the address book from any component. You can select the New Entry icon, Properties icon, Delete icon, or Add to Personal Address Book icon. These will create, modify, or remove an entry or copy it from the currently displayed address book to the Personal Address Book attached to your user profile. See the Store Your Contacts section of this guide to Import a Personal Address Book into Contacts Folder.*

### Create a personal distribution list

1. Ctrl Shift B
2. File, New Entry
3. Select **Personal Distribution List, OK**
4. Type **Name** for group
5. **Add/Remove Members** button
6. Select from **Show Names**
7. `2CLICK` each name to add

---

8. **OK** button

*To address a message to a personal distribution list, select **Personal Address Book** from **Show Names.***

## Set default address book

1. **Tools, Services**

2. **Addressing** tab

3. **Show this address list first** ⊡

*When you open the address book, names in the default address book display.*

## Import a Schedule+ or other
## address book .................. File, Import and Export

*This procedure uses the Import/Export Wizard to import addresses into the Contacts list. You can import from tab- or comma-separated text files, your Personal Address Book, dBase files, and other database programs. Follow instructions on the screen.*

## Download a Microsoft Exchange Server address book

1. **Tools, Synchronize**

2. **Download Address Book**

*Use this procedure to copy new information from the Address Book on the server to the Address Book on your hard disk. You must have the ability to connect to the Exchange server where the address book resides.*

## ARCHIVE AND DELETE ITEMS

*Outlook automatically moves old data to an archive file. You can restore archived data should you ever need to refer to it.*

*By default, Outlook AutoArchives items in Calendar, Tasks, and Journal when they reach six months and Sent and Deleted items when they reach two months. By default, Outlook does not AutoArchive Inbox and Notes items. You cannot AutoArchive Contacts.*

### Enable/disable AutoArchive

1. Tools, Options
2. AutoArchive tab
3. AutoArchive

*Select the **AutoArchive every x days** option to enable AutoArchive, or deselect it to disable AutoArchive. If you enable AutoArchive, specify how often AutoArchive should run, whether or not Outlook should display a prompt before running AutoArchive, and whether or not Outlook should delete rather than archive expired e-mail messages. Unless you specify otherwise, Outlook stores archived items in \My Documents\archive.pst. See the next two procedures to change the default AutoArchive properties for individual folders.*

**Display component folders . . . . . . . . . . . . View, Folder List**
*Display the folder list so that you can set AutoArchive properties for each component.*

**Set AutoArchive properties for each component**

1. `RCLICK` component folder
2. Proper**t**ies
3. AutoArchive tab

*First, display the folder list (**V**iew, **F**older List) or `RCLICK` on the icon in the left panel of the Outlook window. You can archive items in any folder except Contacts.*

*To have Outlook AutoArchive items in this folder, select **C**lean out items. If desired, to delete old items when AutoArchive runs, also select **P**ermanently **d**elete.*

**Exclude selected item from AutoArchive**

1. **F**ile, Proper**t**ies
2. Do not A**u**toArchive this item

**Archive manually** . . . . . . . . . . . . . . . . . . . . . . . . **F**ile, A**r**chive

*You can run AutoArchive at any time, even between scheduled sessions (select **A**rchive all folders according to their AutoArchive settings). AutoArchive must be enabled. Or, run a manual archive (select **Ar**chive this folder and all subfolders).*

**Retrieve an archive**

1. **F**ile, Impor**t** and Export
2. Import from a personal folder (.pst)

*This starts the Import and Export Wizard. Follow screen instructions. Unless you specified otherwise, Outlook stores archived items in \My Documents\archive.pst. The Wizard allows you to select which component folders to restore.*

**Delete an item** . . . . . . . . . . . . . . . . . . . . . . . . **Del** *or* **Ctrl D**
*Outlook moves item to the Deleted Items*
*component.*

**Undo deletion** . . . . . . . . . . . . . . . . . . . . . . . . . . . . **Ctrl Z**
*You must undo deletion before moving to another*
*component. If you have already moved to another*
*component, to undelete an item, cut and paste it from*
*Deleted Items back into its original folder window.*

## MANAGE FILES AND FOLDERS

*File management in Outlook is very much like that in Windows*
*Explorer; you browse the contents of your computer or any*
*connected network drive in windows.*

*Outlook allows you to create personal folders that permit*
*encryption, compression, and password security. Personal*
*folders must contain Outlook items. Remember that a personal*
*folder is different from a normal folder. A normal folder is a*
*subdirectory on a disk, whereas a personal folder is a personal*
*folder file attached to your user profile. Both kinds of folders*
*can appear in the Outlook Bar on the left of the screen.*

*Create and access public folders to share information with*
*other users in a bulletin board format.*

### WORKING WITH FILES AND FOLDERS

**Display folders** . . . . . . . . . . . . . . . . . . . . . . . **View, Folder List**
*The Folder List opens in a separate pane. The*
*Outlook component that you are in remains active on*
*the screen.*

---

**Widen Folder List**. . . . . . . . . . . . . . . . . . . . `DRAG` border

**Connect to network drive** . . . . . **T**ools, **M**ap Network Drive

**Show files and folders** . . . . . . . . . . . . . . . . **G**o, **M**y Computer
*Displays drives, files, and folders in the component
window. The Folder List remains open if you opened it.
Open and close files and folders as in Windows Explorer.
The contents of the Folder List changes to show the
structure of the current directory.*

**Cut, copy, paste, delete, rename** . . . . . . . . . . `RCLICK` icon
*Opens a shortcut menu to move, copy, delete, rename
and otherwise manage files and folders.*

**Create new Office document** . . . . . . . . . . . . . . . . . . . Ctrl N
*This procedure lets you select an Office program
installed on your computer. Files and folders must be
displayed in the component window.*

**Create a folder** . . . . . . . . . . . . . . . . . . . . . . . . . . . Ctrl Shift E

**Find files, folders, or items** . . . . . . . . . . . . . . . . . Ctrl Shift F

## WORKING WITH THE OUTLOOK BAR
*The Outlook Bar is the vertical pane on the left of the
Outlook window. You can add useful folders to this bar.
Groups on the Outlook Bar are headed by buttons such
as Outlook, Mail, and Other.*

### Add folder shortcut to bar

1. `RCLICK` folder icon

2. **A**dd to Outlook Bar
*Adds the folder icon to the group currently displayed in
the Outlook Bar. Usually you place folder shortcuts in
the group displayed when you click*

| Other | in the Outlook Bar. You can rename
this group (see **Rename group**, below). You can create
your own groups and add folder shortcuts. See **Create
new group**, below.

### Remove shortcut from bar

1. `RCLICK` shortcut icon

2. Re**m**ove from Outlook Bar

### Create new group

1. `RCLICK` Bar background

2. **A**dd New Group

3. Type a **name**, **Enter**

### Rename group

1. `RCLICK` group button

2. **R**ename Group

3. Type **name**, **Enter**
For example, `RCLICK` the | Other | button
to rename it "*Project Folders.*"


## CREATING PERSONAL FOLDERS

*A personal folder file can hold (and maintain the organization
of) files from several different subfolders at once; however, it
can only contain Outlook item types. For example, you might
want to create a backup personal folder to contain Inbox,
Contacts, and Notes subfolders.*

*All your personal data from Outlook itself resides in one
personal folder (\Exchange\mailbox.pst).*

*You can specify encryption (encoding so that other programs
cannot read it), compression, and a password.*

---

**Create a personal folder**

1. Tools, Services
2. Add button
3. Select **Personal Folders, OK**
4. Type **drive, path,** and **filename** (e.g., C:\My Documents\backup.pst)
5. Open button
6. Type a new **name** (e.g., Backups), **OK**

*First, open any Outlook component. This procedure creates a personal folder file on your computer's hard disk. You can copy a personal folder file elsewhere on your hard disk, network server, or floppy disk. Personal folder files have a .pst extension.*

**Create a subfolder. . . . . . . . . . . . . . . . . . . . . . . . Ctrl Shift E**

*This procedure creates a folder within another folder (normal folder or personal folder). If you create a folder within a personal folder, you must specify the type of items it can contain (e.g., mail, notes, tasks). When you create a subfolder, it appears on the Outlook Bar.*

**Compact or change password**

1. Tools, Services
2. Select name of folder
3. Properties button

*This procedure lets you compress a personal folder file or change password security for it.*

**Back up a folder**

1. Edit, Copy to Folder

**2.** Select **destination folder, OK**

*First, select items to back up, or use **Ctrl A** to select all items in a folder. This procedure backs up the folder to another components folder. To remind yourself to back up a folder regularly, create a recurring task on your Task list.*

### Move items to a folder

1. **Ctrl Shift V**
2. Select **destination folder, OK**

## CREATING PUBLIC FOLDERS

*A public folder is a bulletin board for multiple users. It can contain forms and documents that users post. Create a public folder for each discussion issue or project. You must have a Microsoft Exchange Server to create and use a public folder. You can also post forms and documents in your Inbox or private folders.*

*Another way to share a document with someone is to link it to a mail message. See the **Insert and Link a Document** procedure in the **Send and Receive Messages** section.*

### Create a public folder

1. **Ctrl Shift E**
2. Type **Name** for folder
3. Select what **Folder contains**
4. Select the parent public folder
5. Type a **Description**

*See your administrator for permission to create a folder in an existing public folder. You can also create a public folder by copying a private folder that already contains items into a public folder.*

---

**View a public folder** . . . . . . . . . . . . Select from Outlook Bar

**Post information**

1. Open public folder

2. **Ctrl Shift S**

*Fill in form and select **Post** button.*

**Post a new document**

1. Open public folder

2. **Ctrl Shift H**

*Select a template and OK, then respond to prompt to either post the document in the current folder or send it to someone. Fill in document and select **Post** button.*

**Post an existing document** . . . . . . . `DRAG` to public folder

## PRINT ITEMS

*An item could be an individual mail message, task, appointment or other data created in Outlook. You can print individual items or entire views.*

*From the Print dialog box, select the print style associated with the view you want to print. If you want to print a single item, select the Memo print style. You cannot print icon or timeline views.*

*You can modify, but not delete default print styles. All print styles include the date, your name, and the page number in the footer.*

**Set print layout** . . . . . . . . . . . . . . . . . . . . . . . . . File, Page Setup

**Preview printout** . . . . . . . . . . . . . . . . . . . . . . . . . . . . . . Ctrl F2

**Zoom in/out in preview** . . . . . . . . . . . . . . . . . . . . . . `CLICK`

**Exit preview** . . . . . . . . . . . . . . . . . . . . . . . . . . . . . . . . **Esc**

**Print and set print options** . . . . . . . . . . . . . . . . . . . . . **Ctrl P**
*Displays the Print dialog box where you select a print
style and can preview the results. Remember that the
Memo style prints one item per page.*

**Print using default print settings** . . . . . . . . . . . . . . . . . 🖨
*Prints without displaying the Print dialog box.*

## MANAGE ADD-INS

*Add-ins help you use Outlook with other mail programs and
servers and provides you with more Outlook options.*

*Add-in files have an .ecf extension that stands for Extension
Configuration File.*

### Install and load an add-in

1. <u>T</u>ools, <u>O</u>ptions
2. **General** tab
3. **A<u>d</u>d-In Manager** button
4. **<u>I</u>nstall** button
5. Select add-in to install
6. **<u>O</u>pen** button

*To load the add-in, select its checkbox in the Add-In
Manager. If the add-in you wish to install does not
appear, use the Add/Remove Programs icon in
Window's Control Panel to add the add-in to
Outlook (if you installed Outlook individually) or to
Microsoft Office.*

**cc:Mail Menu Extension** . . . . . . . . . . . . . . . . . . . . . **Ccmxp.ecf**
*Add cc:Mail to the list of available information
services.*

---

**Delegate Access** . . . . . . . . . . . . . . . . . . . . . . . . . **Dlgsetp.ecf**
*Adds **Delegates** tab to **Tools, Options**.*

**Digital Security** . . . . . . . . . . . . . . . . . . . . . . . . . **Etexch.ecf**
*Adds **Security** tab to **Tools, Options** for digital
signature and message sealing. You must be
connected to a Microsoft Exchange Server that stores
the Key Management Security database.*

**Exchange Extensions** . . . . . . . . . . . . . . . . . . . . . **Emsuix.ecf**
*Adds **Out of Office Assistant** and **Inbox Assistant** to
**Tools** menu and adds Remote Mail settings to the
Mail icon in Windows' Control Panel. Available only if
Microsoft Exchange Server is installed.*

**Internet Mail** . . . . . . . . . . . . . . . . . . . . . . . . . . . **Minet.ecf**
*Adds Internet mail to the list of available information
services.*

**Mail 3.0 Extensions** . . . . . . . . . . . . . . . . . . . . . . **Mail3.ecf**
*Enables Outlook to use extensions created in Mail
3.0.*

**Microsoft Fax** . . . . . . . . . . . . . . . . . . . . . . . . . . . **Awfext.ecf**
*If you have previously installed Microsoft Fax, this
adds Microsoft At Work fax software to the list of
available information services.*

**Microsoft Mail 3.x Menu Extensions** . . . . . . . . . **Msfsmenu.ecf**
*Enables Outlook to use menu extensions created in
Microsoft Mail 3.x.*

**Microsoft Mail 3.x Property
Sheet Extensions**...................... **Msfsprop.ecf**
*Enables Outlook to use dialog box extensions created
in Microsoft Mail 3.x.*

**Schedule+**............................ **Msspc.ecf**
*Provides Schedule+ compatibility.*

**The Microsoft Network**.................. **Msn.ecf**
*Adds Microsoft Network to the list of available
information services.*

# Shortcut Reference

This section of the guide is a reference tool.

Use the index and table of contents to find the exact shortcut you need. Since this section is organized by major menu choices, you will also find shortcuts organized in simple, easy-to-grasp categories.

In addition to specific shortcut keys, procedures give you relevant, related information. For example, you will learn where the cursor should be before the shortcut, and you will learn what to expect once you select the shortcut.

Learn as many shortcuts as you can to become a true Outlook expert!

## OUTLOOK SHORTCUTS

### GETTING HELP
*The Office Assistant offers help, messages, tips, and reminders.*

**Get help on option** ......................... Shift F1
*First, highlight dialog box option or command to*
*show pop-up ScreenTip.*

**Start help** ...................................... F1
*This starts the Office Assistant or Contents and Index*
*depending on your Help setting (see the **Open the***
***Assistant or the Index when you press F1** procedure*
*in the **Office Assistant** section).*

**Make Office Assistant balloon active** ............. Alt F6
*Press to move between Outlook and the balloon.*

**Close help message or balloon** .................... Esc

**View a tip.** ............... CLICK light bulb in Assistant
*A light bulb appears when the Assistant can offer*
*effective ways to perform a task. If the Office*
*Assistant is not visible, click the Office Assistant tool*
*in the toolbar when a light bulb appears in the tool.*

**Next tip** ..................................... Alt N

**Previous tip** ................................. Alt B

**Close tips** .................................... Esc

## MENUS

Menu bar (on/off) . . . . . . . . . . . . . . . . . . . . . . . . . . . . Alt *or* F10

Control menu . . . . . . . . . . . . . . . . . . . . . . . . . . . . . Alt Spacebar

Windows Start menu . . . . . . . . . . . . . . . . . . . . . . . . . . Ctrl Esc

Shortcut menu . . . . . . . . . . . . . . . . . . . . . . . . . . . . . . . Shift F10
*Or,* ▮ RCLICK *the item.*

Format menu . . . . . . . . . . . . . . . . . . . . . . . . . . . . . . . . . Alt O
*When working in an item. Use the Format menu for
character and paragraph formatting.*

First command. . . . . . . . . . . . . . . . . . . . . . . . . . . . . . . . Home
*First, press* **Alt** *to activate menu.*

Last command . . . . . . . . . . . . . . . . . . . . . . . . . . . . . . . . End
*First, press* **Alt** *to activate menu.*

Activate menu and command . . . . . . . . Alt *underlined letter*
*You can press and release* **Alt,** *or hold it down while
pressing the underlined letter. Every menu command
has an underlined "hot key" that you can use to select
the command.*

Close menu completely . . . . . . . . . . . . . . . . . . . . . Alt *or* F10

Close submenu only. . . . . . . . . . . . . . . . . . . . . . . . . . . . Esc

## TOOLBARS

Activate menu . . . . . . . . . . . . . . . . . . . . . . . . . . . . Alt *or* F10

Switch to toolbar (from menu). . . . . . . . . . . . . . . . Ctrl Tab

Next button. . . . . . . . . . . . . . . . . . . . . . . . . . . . . . . . . . . Tab

Previous button. . . . . . . . . . . . . . . . . . . . . . . . . . . . . . Shift Tab

Activate button. . . . . . . . . . . . . . . . . . . . . . . . . . . . . . . . Enter

## WORKING IN DIALOG BOXES

Go to next tab in dialog box. . . . . . . . . . . . . . . . . . Ctrl Tab

Previous tab. . . . . . . . . . . . . . . . . . . . . . . . . . . . . Ctrl Shift Tab

Next option (or option group). . . . . . . . . . . . . . . . . . . . . Tab

Previous option (or option group). . . . . . . . . . . Shift Tab

Select/clear a check box. . . . . . . . . . . . . . . . . . . . . Spacebar

Select/clear option . . . . . . . . . . . . . . . . . Alt underlined letter

## WORKING IN DATE NAVIGATOR

*The Date Navigator is a small monthly calendar that appears
when you need to select a date.*

First day of week. . . . . . . . . . . . . . . . . . . . . . . . . . . Alt Home

Last day of week . . . . . . . . . . . . . . . . . . . . . . . . . . . . . Alt End

Previous week. . . . . . . . . . . . . . . . . . . . . . . . . . . . . . . . . Alt ↑

Next week. . . . . . . . . . . . . . . . . . . . . . . . . . . . . . . . . . . . . Alt ↓

Previous month. . . . . . . . . . . . . . . . . . . . . . . . . . . . Alt PgUp

Next month . . . . . . . . . . . . . . . . . . . . . . . . . . . . . . . Alt PgDn

Remove one day from selection . . . . . . . . . . . . . . . . Alt ←

Add one day to selection . . . . . . . . . . . . . . . . . . . . . . Alt →

## WORKING IN DAY/WEEK/MONTH VIEW

View 1-9 (x) days in window . . . . . . . . . . . . . . . . . . . . . . . Alt x
*For example, Alt 2 shows two days on the screen.*
*View up to 9 days (Alt 9). In day/week/month view.*

View 10 days . . . . . . . . . . . . . . . . . . . . . . . . . . . . . . . . . . Alt 0 *(zero)*

View weeks . . . . . . . . . . . . . . . . . . . . . . . . . . . . . . . . . . . Alt -

View months . . . . . . . . . . . . . . . . . . . . . . . . . . . . . . . . . . . Alt =

Go between Calendar/TaskPad/Folder List . . . . . . . . . . . . F6

Previous appointment . . . . . . . . . . . . . . . . . . . . . . . . . . Shift Tab

Next appointment . . . . . . . . . . . . . . . . . . . . . . . . . . . . . . . Tab

First hour . . . . . . . . . . . . . . . . . . . . . . . . . . . . . . . . . . . . . Home

Last hour . . . . . . . . . . . . . . . . . . . . . . . . . . . . . . . . . . . . . End

Beginning of week . . . . . . . . . . . . . . . . . . . . . . . . . . . . . Home

End of week . . . . . . . . . . . . . . . . . . . . . . . . . . . . . . . . . . . End

Previous day . . . . . . . . . . . . . . . . . . . . . . . . . . . . . . . . . . . ←

Next day . . . . . . . . . . . . . . . . . . . . . . . . . . . . . . . . . . . . . . →

Previous week . . . . . . . . . . . . . . . . . . . . . . . . . . Alt ↑ *or* PgUp

Next week . . . . . . . . . . . . . . . . . . . . . . . . . . . . Alt ↓ *or* PgDn

Previous month . . . . . . . . . . . . . . . . . . . . . . . . . . . . Alt PgUp

Next month . . . . . . . . . . . . . . . . . . . . . . . . . . . . . . . Alt PgDn

Move appointment to another day . . . . . . . . . . . Alt ↑↓←→
*Use this procedure in Month View or Week View or*
*when displaying more than one day in Day view.*

**Move appointment within a day** . . . . . . . . . . . . . . . . . Alt ↑↓
*Use this procedure in Day View.*

## WORKING IN CARD VIEW

*A card is a view of all fields within an item. For example, in
Contacts, you can view address cards. To change to a different
view, use View, Current View.*

**Previous card** . . . . . . . . . . . . . . . . . . . . . . . . . . . . . . . . . . . ↑

**Next card** . . . . . . . . . . . . . . . . . . . . . . . . . . . . . . . . . . . . . . . ↓

**Closest card in next column** . . . . . . . . . . . . . . . . . . . . . . . →

**Closest card in previous column** . . . . . . . . . . . . . . . . . . . ←

**First card in list** . . . . . . . . . . . . . . . . . . . . . . . . . . . . . . . Home

**Last card in list** . . . . . . . . . . . . . . . . . . . . . . . . . . . . . . . . End

**First card on first page** . . . . . . . . . . . . . . . . . . . . . . . . PgUp

**First card on last page** . . . . . . . . . . . . . . . . . . . . . . . . PgDn

**Select specific card(s)** . . . . . . . . . . . . . . . . . . . . Type letters
*Type one or more letters of the card's name or
sorted field. Or select an alphabetical tab on the right
of the screen.*

**Select/unselect current card** . . . . . . . . . . . . . . . Ctrl Spacebar
*Or, click the card's heading.*

**Select multiple cards** . . . . . . . . . . . . . . . Ctrl **CLICK** items

**Select multiple cards in order** . . . . . . . . . . . . . . . . . Shift ↑/↓

**Select all cards** . . . . . . . . . . . . . . . . . . . . . . . . . . . . . . . . Ctrl A

**Select a field** .......................... `CLICK` field
*If you select a field in this way, you can edit the field.*

**Move to a field** ............................ **F2** *twice*
*The card remains selected, but you can use the arrow*
*keys to highlight a field to modify.*

**Next field** ......................... **Tab** *or* **Enter** *or* ↓

**Previous field** .............. **Shift Tab** *or* **Shift Enter** *or* ↑

**Edit a field (on/off)** .............................. **F2**

### WORKING IN TABLE VIEW

*A table is a grid of rows and columns. Each item occupies a*
*row and each field appears below a column heading. For*
*example, show mail messages or tasks in a table. To change to*
*a different view, use **View, Current View.***

**Previous item** ................................... ↑

**Next item** ...................................... ↓

**First item** .................................. **Home**

**Last item** ..................................... **End**

**Item at top of screen** ......................... **PgUp**

**Next screenful of items** ....................... **PgDn**

**Select/unselect current item** ............... **Ctrl Spacebar**

**Select multiple items** ............... **Ctrl** `CLICK` items

**Select multiple items in order** ................. **Shift** ↑/↓

**Select all items in folder** ....................... **Ctrl A**

## EDITING ITEMS

Save ........................................ Ctrl S

Save and close ............................. Alt S

Save as ..................................... F12

Create new item............................. Ctrl N
*First, open the component for the item that you wish
to create. For example, to use Ctrl N to create a new
journal entry, first open the Journal window.*

Open item.............. `2CLICK` *or* Enter *or* Ctrl O

Delete item(s)........................ Del *or* Ctrl D

Move item(s) to another folder ............. Ctrl Shift V

Copy item(s) to another folder ............. Ctrl Shift Y

Cut item(s) to Clipboard ..................... Ctrl X

Copy item(s) to Clipboard ..................... Ctrl C

Paste cut or copied item...................... Ctrl V
*This procedure pastes contents of Clipboard.*

Undo..................... Alt Backspace *or* Ctrl Z
*You can no longer undo an edit if you switch to
another Outlook component. You cannot undo all
actions.*

## EDITING FIELDS IN ITEMS

Find text..................................... F4
*This procedure finds text in a text (comment) box.*

**Find next** . . . . . . . . . . . . . . . . . . . . . . . . . . . . . . . **Shift F4**
*Repeats the last find.*

**Select all** . . . . . . . . . . . . . . . . . . . . . . . . . . . . . . . . **Ctrl A**

**Cut text/object to Clipboard** . . . . . . . . . **Shift Del** *or* **Ctrl X**

**Copy text/object to Clipboard** . . . . . . . . **Ctrl Ins** *or* **Ctrl C**

**Paste from Clipboard** . . . . . . . . . . . . . . . . **Shift Ins** *or* **Ctrl V**

**Delete selection** . . . . . . . . . . . . . . . . . . . . . . **Del** *or* **Ctrl D**

**Undo** . . . . . . . . . . . . . . . . . . . . . . . . **Alt Backspace** *or* **Ctrl Z**

**Spell check** . . . . . . . . . . . . . . . . . . . . . . . . . . . . . . . . . . **F7**
*This procedure checks spelling in a text (comment)*
*box.*

**Cancel spell check** . . . . . . . . . . . . . . . . . . . . . . . . . . . **Esc**

**FORMATTING TEXT**
*You can format text in a text (comment) box.*

**Open Format menu** . . . . . . . . . . . . . . . . . . . . . . . . . . . **Alt O**

**Show/hide Formatting**
**toolbar** . . . . . . . . . . . . . **RCLICK** toolbar area background
*Position the mouse pointer at the top of the screen in*
*a blank area to the right of the menu or toolbar.*

**Change case of selected text** . . . . . . . . . . . . . . . . . . **Shift F3**

**Boldface** . . . . . . . . . . . . . . . . . . . . . . . . . . . . . . . . . . . . **Ctrl B**

**Italics** . . . . . . . . . . . . . . . . . . . . . . . . . . . . . . . . . . . . . . **Ctrl I**

**Underline** . . . . . . . . . . . . . . . . . . . . . . . . . . . . . . . . . . . **Ctrl U**

**Larger font** . . . . . . . . . . . . . . . . . . . . . . . . . . . . . . . . . . **Ctrl ]**

| | |
|---|---|
| Smaller font ..................................... | Ctrl [ |
| Remove font formatting ................... | Ctrl Spacebar |
| Bullets (on/off)................................ | Ctrl Shift L |
| Center ............................................ | Ctrl E |
| Left-align........................................ | Ctrl L |
| Indent............................................. | Ctrl T |
| Decrease indent ............................. | Ctrl Shift T |

## CONTACTS

| | |
|---|---|
| Create a contact............................. | Ctrl Shift C |
| Create a contact from Contacts .......... | Ctrl N |
| Dial a Contact ............................... | Ctrl Shift D |

## MAIL

| | |
|---|---|
| Go to Inbox ................................... | Ctrl Shift I |
| Go to Outbox ................................ | Ctrl Shift O |
| Create a message............................ | Ctrl Shift M |
| Create a message from Mail............... | Ctrl N |
| Send message ............................... | Ctrl Enter |
| Check for new mail (not headers) ................. | F5 |

*Use this procedure if you wish to transfer all
messages to your computer and delete them from the
mail delivery service's computer. If you share a
mailbox with another user or use two or more
computers, do not use this command.*

| | |
|---|---|
| Post a file (Microsoft Exchange only) ............... | Alt P |

*Post an Office file in a public folder used as a bulletin
board on a Microsoft Exchange Server.*

Open Address Book . . . . . . . . . . . . . . . . . . . . . . . Ctrl Shift B

Reply to message. . . . . . . . . . . . . . . . . . . . . . . . . . . . Ctrl R

Reply to sender and all recipients . . . . . . . . . . . Ctrl Shift R

Forward message. . . . . . . . . . . . . . . . . . . . . . . . . . . . Ctrl F

Mark message as read . . . . . . . . . . . . . . . . . . . . . . Ctrl Q

Check names (not in WordMail) . . . . . . . . . . . . . . . Ctrl K
*Checks that names you type in recipient fields (To:,
Cc:, and Bcc:) are correctly entered before sending mail
if automatic name checking is disabled (**Tools**, **Options**,
**Automatic Name Checking**).*

Check names in WordMail. . . . . . . . . . . . . . . . . . . . . Alt K
*This procedure checks that names you type in
recipient fields (To:, Cc:, and Bcc) are correctly
entered before sending mail if you have automatic
name checking disabled (**Tools**, **Options**, **Sending** tab,
**Automatic Name Checking**).*

## CALENDAR

Create an appointment . . . . . . . . . . . . . . . . . . . . Ctrl Shift C

Create an appointment from Calendar . . . . . . . . . . . Ctrl N

Create a meeting request . . . . . . . . . . . . . . . . . . Ctrl Shift Q

## NOTES

Create a note. . . . . . . . . . . . . . . . . . . . . . . . . . . . . Ctrl Shift N

Create a note from Notes. . . . . . . . . . . . . . . . . . . . . Ctrl N

## TASKS

Create a task. . . . . . . . . . . . . . . . . . . . . . . . . . . . . Ctrl Shift K

Create a task from Tasks. . . . . . . . . . . . . . . . . . . . . Ctrl N

Create a task request. . . . . . . . . . . . . . . . . . . . . . Ctrl Shift U

## JOURNAL

Create a journal entry........................ Ctrl Shift J

Create a journal entry from Journal .............. Ctrl N

Create a journal entry for the selected or open item ... Ctrl J

*Creates a journal entry with information about the item filled in for you. For example, if you create a journal entry for the selected mail message, the entry includes recipient or sender, subject, and a shortcut icon to the message.*

## FILES AND FOLDERS

Find file, folder, or Outlook item...................... F3

Create a folder............................. Ctrl Shift E

Go to folder.................................. Ctrl Y

Refresh folder.................................. F5

*If changes to files and folders such as renaming or copying do not appear on the screen, refresh it.*

## PRINT PREVIEW

Switch to print preview ........................ Ctrl F2

Zoom....................................... Alt Z

Previous page................................. PgUp

Next page ................................... PgDn

Top....................................... Home

Bottom .................................... End

Go to Print dialog box........................... Alt P

Go to Page Setup dialog box ...................... Alt S

Close print preview ............................ Esc

## Outlook is More than an E-mail System

Even if you already have an e-mail service or if you do not use e-mail, you can still put Outlook to work in its capacity as a personal information manager. Use it to schedule your appointments, keep notes, list tasks, track your work history, and other management tasks.

## Each Component has Several Views

Use the **View, Current View** command to view your mail, calendar, and other Outlook components from a fresh angle.

## Categories Help You Cross-Reference

As you set up Outlook, consider creating personal categories for Outlook items. You can assign several categories to an item. This helps you look up related items, no matter what folder contains them. You can view related items using the **View, Current View, By Category** command within any Outlook component. Or, use **Ctrl Shift F** to find all items related to a category.

## Archiving Helps You Clean Up

Depending on how you use it, Outlook can generate a great deal of data. Use AutoArchive and manual archiving to automatically delete and/or archive old data.

## Maximize the Outlook Window

Double-click on the Outlook window's title bar to maximize the window's size. You can view much more information this way. The only problem this causes is it obscures Notes that you have opened.

## You Can Display Several Components at Once

Right-click the component such as Calendar or Notes in the Outlook Bar or component's title bar and select **Open in New Window**. The new window eliminates the Outlook Bar. You can use the **View** command to hide the Status bar and Toolbars as well. Open all desired components in this way and then minimize the Outlook program window. To tile the non-minimized windows neatly, right-click Windows' Taskbar background and select **Cascade, Tile Horizontally,** or **Tile Vertically.** Notes do not tile in this way.

## Turn on Your Modem

If your modem is not connected and turned on, you will receive constant, irritating reminders that Outlook cannot initialize it.

## Checking Mail Wipes out Your Mailbox

If you share a mailbox with another person or if you access the mailbox from several different computers, you need to be careful about how you check your mail. Use the **Tools, Remote Mail, Connect, Do only the following** command, rather than the **F5** key, and download headers only. When you are offline, you can mark the headers of mail messages you want to receive or of which you want to receive copies. Then use **Tools, Remote Mail, Connect, Do only the following** again to retrieve the messages whose headers you marked.

## Quickly Sort Items by Column Heading

Click on a column heading in any table view to sort items by that column. Click again for a reverse sort.

## The Outlook Bar is Flexible

The Outlook Bar is the vertical pane located on the left side of the Outlook window. You can add shortcuts to important folders to the Outlook Bar. In addition, you can create and rename group buttons on the Outlook Bar. You can hide the Outlook Bar altogether with the **View, Outlook Bar** command.

## Some Features are Dimmed

Some features such as Out of Office Assistant, Inbox Assistant, digital signatures, message sealing, and file posting are available only if you are connected to a Microsoft Exchange Server.

## NOTES

## QUICK LIST OF SHORTCUTS

Start from desktop . . . . . . . . . . . . . . . . . . . . . . . . `2CLICK` Outlook icon
   Start from menu . . . . . . . . . . . . . . . . Ctrl Esc, P, Microsoft Outlook
   Exit . . . . . . . . . . . . . . . . . . . . . . . . . . . . . . . . . . . . . . . . . . Alt F4
View Inbox . . . . . . . . . . . . . . . . . . . . . . . . . . . . . . . . . . . . Ctrl Shift I
   View Outbox . . . . . . . . . . . . . . . . . . . . . . . . . . . . . . . . . Ctrl Shift O
Create a category . . . . . . . . . . . . . . . . . . . . . . . . . . . . . . Alt EI Alt M
   Assign item to category(s) . . . . . . . . . . . . . . . . `RCLICK` item, I
   See items in category . . . . . . . . . . . . . Ctrl Shift F, More Choices
Create an appointment . . . . . . . . . . . . . . . . . . . . . . . . . . . Ctrl Shift K
   Create a appointment from Calendar . . . . . . . . . . . . . . . . . . Ctrl N
   Create a recurring appointment . . . . . . . . . . . . . . . . . . . . . . Alt CA
   View days, weeks, months . . . . . . . . . . . . . . . . . . . . Alt 1-9 0-=
   Go to a day . . . . . . . . . . . . . . . . . . . . . . . . . . . . . . . . . . . . Ctrl G
   Previous/next appointment . . . . . . . . . . . . . . . . . . . . Shift Tab/Tab
   Previous/next day . . . . . . . . . . . . . . . . . . . . . . . . . . . . . . . ←→
   Previous/next week . . . . . . . . . . . . . . . . . . Alt ↑/↓ or PgUp/PgDn
   Previous/next month . . . . . . . . . . . . . . . . . . . Alt PgUp/Alt PgDn
Schedule meeting from Calendar . . . . . . . . . . . . . . . . . . Ctrl Shift Q
   Schedule a recurring meeting . . . . . . . . . . . . . . . . . . . . . . . Alt CC
   Reschedule (notifies others) . . . . . . . . . . `DRAG` appointment
   Cancel meeting (notifies others) . . . . . . . . . . . . . . . . . . . . . . Ctrl D
Create an event (e.g., trade show, trip) . . . . . . . . . . . . . . . . . Alt CE
   Create recurring event (e.g., birthday) . . . . . . . . . . . . . . . . . Alt CV
   Add national holidays . . . . . . . . . . . . . . Alt TO, Calendar tab, Alt H
   View all events or annual events . . . . . . . . . . . . . . . . . . . . . Alt VV
Create a contact . . . . . . . . . . . . . . . . . . . . . . . . . . . . . . . . Ctrl Shift C
   Sort contacts . . . . . . . . . . . . . . Alt VR or `CLICK` column header
   Find a contact . . . . . . . . . . . . . . . . . . . . . . . . . . . . . . . . Ctrl Shift F
Call a contact (AutoDial) . . . . . . . . . . . . . . . . . . . . . . . . . . . Alt TD
   Call a non-contact . . . . . . . . . . . . . . . . . . . . . . . . . . . . Ctrl Shift D
   Redial . . . . . . . . . . . . . . . . . . . . . . . . . . . . . . . . . . . . . . . Alt TDR
   Schedule meeting with contact . . . . . . . . . . . . . . . . . . . Ctrl Shift G
   Send message . . . . . . . . . . . . . . . . . . . . . . . . . . . . . . . . . Alt OM
   Create letter . . . . . . . . . . . . . . . . . . . . . . . . . . . . . . . . . . . Alt OL
Create a task . . . . . . . . . . . . . . . . . . . . . . . . . . . . . . . . . . Ctrl Shift K
   Schedule task . . . . . . . . . . . . . . . . `DRAG` task icon to Calendar icon
   View active, overdue, or upcoming tasks . . . . . . . . . . . . . . . . Alt VV
   Mark task as complete . . . . . . . . . . . . . . . . . . `CLICK` check field
   View tasks you have assigned . . . . . . . . . . . . . . Alt VV, Assignment
Create a note . . . . . . . . . . . . . . . . . . . . . . . . . . . . . . . . . . Ctrl Shift N
   E-mail a note . . . . . . . . . . . . . . . . . . . . . . . . . . . . . . . . . . . Ctrl F

| | |
|---|---|
| Set note defaults. . . . . . . . . . . . . . . . . . . . . . . . . . . . | Alt TO, Tasks/Notes tab |
| Delete a note. . . . . . . . . . . . . . . . . . . . . . . . . . . . . . . | Del |
| Open address book . . . . . . . . . . . . . . . . . . . . . . . . . . | Ctrl Shift B |
| Use address book and create message. . . . . . . . | New Message button |
| Use address book and create an entry. . . . . . . . . . | New Entry button |
| Create fax or e-mail. . . . . . . . . . . . . . . . . . . . . . . . . | Ctrl Shift M |
| Create fax or e-mail from Mail. . . . . . . . . . . . . . . . . | Ctrl N |
| Create using template . . . . . . . . . . . . . . . . . . . . . . | Alt MH |
| Create from Address Book. . . . . . . . . . . . . . . . . . | New Message button |
| Create and send a document . . . . . . . . . . . . . . . . | Ctrl Shift H |
| Create fax . . . . . . . . . . . . . . . . . . . . . . . . . . . . . . . . | Alt MX |
| Fax a document. . . . . . . . . . . . . . . | **RCLICK** file, N, Fax Recipient |
| E-mail a file . . . . . . . . . . . . . . . . . . | **RCLICK** file, N, Mail Recipient |
| Attach file to fax or e-mail. . . . . . . . . . . . . . . . . . . . | Alt IF |
| Download new mail . . . . . . . . . . . . . . . . . . . . . . . . . | Ctrl M *or* F5 |
| Reply to sender. . . . . . . . . . . . . . . . . . . . . . . . . . . . | Ctrl R |
| Reply to sender and all recipients . . . . . . . . . . . . | Ctrl Shift R |
| Forward a message . . . . . . . . . . . . . . . . . . . . . . . . | Ctrl F |
| Select all. . . . . . . . . . . . . . . . . . . . . . . . . . . . . . . . . | Ctrl A |
| Select several. . . . . . . . . . . . . . . . . . . . . . . . . . . . | Ctrl **CLICK** |
| Save item . . . . . . . . . . . . . . . . . . . . . . . . . . . . . . . . | Ctrl S |
| Save and close. . . . . . . . . . . . . . . . . . . . . . . . . . . . | Alt S |
| Save as . . . . . . . . . . . . . . . . . . . . . . . . . . . . . . . . . | F12 |
| Create new item . . . . . . . . . . . . . . . . . . . . . . . . . . . | Ctrl N |
| Open item. . . . . . . . . . . . . . . . . . . **2CLICK** *or* Enter *or* Ctrl O |
| Delete item. . . . . . . . . . . . . . . . . . . . . . . . . . . . . | Del *or* Ctrl D |
| Cut item (or text). . . . . . . . . . . . . . . . . . . . . . . . . . . | Ctrl X |
| Copy item (or text) . . . . . . . . . . . . . . . . . . . . . . . . . | Ctrl C |
| Paste item (or text) . . . . . . . . . . . . . . . . . . . . . . . . . | Ctrl V |
| Move item to another folder. . . . . . . . . . . . . . . . . . | Ctrl Shift V |
| Copy item to another folder. . . . . . . . . . . . . . . . . . | Ctrl Shift Y |
| Undo . . . . . . . . . . . . . . . . . . . . . . . . . | Alt Backspace *or* Ctrl Z |
| Open Format menu. . . . . . . . . . . . . . . . . . . . . . . . . | Alt O |
| Boldface. . . . . . . . . . . . . . . . . . . . . . . . . . . . . . . . . | Ctrl B |
| Italics . . . . . . . . . . . . . . . . . . . . . . . . . . . . . . . . . . . | Ctrl I |
| Underline . . . . . . . . . . . . . . . . . . . . . . . . . . . . . . . . | Ctrl U |
| Larger font . . . . . . . . . . . . . . . . . . . . . . . . . . . . . . . | Ctrl ] |
| Smaller font . . . . . . . . . . . . . . . . . . . . . . . . . . . . . . | Ctrl [ |
| Remove font formatting . . . . . . . . . . . . . . . . . . . . | Ctrl Spacebar |
| Bullets (on/off) . . . . . . . . . . . . . . . . . . . . . . . . . . . . | Ctrl Shift L |
| Center. . . . . . . . . . . . . . . . . . . . . . . . . . . . . . . . . . . | Ctrl E |
| Left-align. . . . . . . . . . . . . . . . . . . . . . . . . . . . . . . . . | Ctrl L |
| Indent . . . . . . . . . . . . . . . . . . . . . . . . . . . . . . . . . . | Ctrl T |
| Decrease indent . . . . . . . . . . . . . . . . . . . . . . . . . . | Ctrl Shift T |

|     | F1 | F2 | F3 | F4 |
|-----|----|----|----|----|
| C+S |    |    |    |    |
| C   |    | Preview |    |    |
| A   |    |    |    | Exit Outlook |
| S   | What Is? |    | Change Case | Find Next |
| U   | Help | Edit Field On/Off | Find Files | Find Text/List |

|     | F1 | F2 | F3 | F4 |
|-----|----|----|----|----|
| C+S |    | Next Window |    |    |
| C   |    |    |    |    |
| A   |    | Switch to Folders |    |    |
| S   |    | Previous Pane |    |    |
| U   | Refresh/Download | Next Pane | Spell Check |    |

|     | F1 | F2 | F3 | F4 |
|-----|----|----|----|----|
| C+S |    |    |    |    |
| C   |    |    |    |    |
| A   |    |    |    |    |
| S   |    | Shortcut Menu |    | Save |
| U   |    | Menu |    | Save As |

C+S = CTRL + SHIFT    C = CTRL    A = ALT    S = SHIFT    U = UNSHIFT